Rose Elliot's Book of Vegetables

Rose Elliot is the author of several bestselling cookbooks, and is renowned for her practical and creative approach. She writes regularly for the *Vegetarian* and has contributed to national newspapers and magazines as well as broadcasting on radio and television. She is married and has three children.

D0589644

Other titles available in the series

Rose Elliot's Book of Breads
Rose Elliot's Book of Fruits
Rose Elliot's Book of Salads

Rose Elliot's Book of

Vegetables

Fontana Paperbacks

First published by Fontana Paperbacks 1983

Set in 10 on 11pt Linotron Plantin
Illustrations by Vana Haggerty
Made and printed in Great Britain by
William Collins Sons & Co. Ltd, Glasgow

Introduction

Well-cooked vegetables can add so much to a meal, lifting it from the ordinary to the luxury class. And there's never been a better time for the vegetable cook. The range available has increased greatly over recent years and modern transporting methods mean they're fresher when they reach the shops. Vegetables such as aubergines and peppers, which used to be quite difficult to get, can now be bought in any town, while more unusual ones such as salsify and okra are appearing alongside the swedes and turnips.

This book is about cooking such less familiar vegetables as well as making the most of the more common ones.

BASIC PREPARATION

Choose small, tender vegetables which are bright and firm and look vital and full of life.

Allow 175 g (6 oz) vegetables per person (weighed before preparation), or 225 g (8 oz) where there is a lot of waste, as in leafy leeks and also spinach, and 450 g (1 lb) for peas and beans in their pods.

Store vegetables in a cool place (the bottom of the fridge is ideal), and use them as soon as you can.

Cut away as little as possible when preparing the vegetables, but see that ones which will cook together are about the same size: cut larger ones if necessary.

BASIC COOKING

The basic method of cooking, and the one which is suitable for nearly all vegetables is boiling (I have described other methods in the recipes and Alphabetical Guide, pages 8–13, where they apply).

Boiling means plunging the prepared vegetables into lightly salted boiling water, letting them boil vigorously until just tender, then draining immediately.

It's important to make sure the water has reached a rolling boil before adding the vegetables. The exception to this is root vegetables which can be started with either boiling or cold water. Root vegetables should be boiled in enough water to cover them, with a lid on the pan.

Other vegetables can either be cooked conservatively; that is, put into just enough boiling water to prevent them from boiling dry (about 1 cm/½ in for 700-900 g/1½-2 lb); or plunged into a large pan three-quarters full of boiling water, which is the chef's method. The pan should be uncovered.

Whichever method you use, keep testing the vegetables by piercing them with a sharp pointed knife. The moment they feel tender but still a bit resistant, remove them from the heat immediately and drain thoroughly.

A variation of boiling is steaming. Here the vegetables are set above the water in a perforated steamer saucepan, metal colander or steaming basket so that they cook in the steam without touching the water. This is a good method for root vegetables and delicate ones such as asparagus. It's best for small quantities of vegetables because if you have too many they will not cook evenly.

FLAVOURING AND SERVING

Fresh vegetables that are well cooked are good enough to serve as they are, but are enhanced by a swirl of butter and a grating of black pepper. Chopped fresh herbs, snipped over the vegetables just before serving, are delicious, and spices are useful for adding variety to the more common vegetables. Dairy products such as cheese, soured cream and yoghurt complement vegetables particularly well and add extra nourishment. In addition to this, vegetables can be coated in crisp batter, mashed to a creamy purée or made into croquettes and bakes. There's plenty of scope for imagination and creativity. The recipes in this book contain some ideas, but first here is a guide to the basic preparation and cooking of specific types of vegetables.

An Alphabetical Guide to Preparing and Cooking Vegetables

Artichokes, globe Allow one per person; break off stem level with base. Snip off the points of the leaves. Wash artichokes well. Immerse artichokes in boiling water to cover (use an enamel or stainless steel saucepan) and boil for 30-45 minutes, until a leaf pulls off easily. Turn artichokes upside down to drain. Serve with melted butter.

Artichokes, Jerusalem Peel, then boil in an enamel or stainless steel pan for 20-40 minutes, until tender. Or cook in butter as described on page 15.

Asparagus Break off thick stalk ends; peel upwards to make base the same width as upper stem. Tie stems in a bundle, stand in 2 cm (1 in) boiling water. Cover pan with a dome of foil if necessary. Boil for 8-12 minutes, until tender. Serve with melted butter or a creamy sauce.

Aubergines Slice or cube, with or without peeling. Sprinkle with salt and leave in a colander under a weight for 30 minutes, then rinse to remove bitter liquid. Squeeze dry, fry in oil for about 5 minutes until tender.

Beansprouts Wash, drain and stir-fry in 1-2 tablespoons oil for 1-2 minutes. Best included in a mixture of stir-fried vegetables as on page 19.

Beetroot Cut off the leaves, if still attached, 10 cm (4 in) above the beetroot. Do not peel or cut the beet or the colour will come out. Boil in water to cover, with a lid on the pan, for 1-3 hours. Slip off the skins, slice or cube the beetroot, re-heat in butter or a sauce: (page 20).

Broad beans Prepare and cook tiny ones like French beans. Remove older beans from the pod, then boil in a large panful of unsalted boiling water for 5-10 minutes. Drain and serve with butter and chopped herbs.

Broccoli and calabrese Prepare stems as for asparagus. Boil for 5-7 minutes until just tender. Drain and serve with melted butter or a rich sauce.

Brussels sprouts Choose small firm ones. Trim off outer leaves and stalk ends. Cook really tiny ones whole; halve or quarter larger ones. Boil quickly until just tender: 2-5 minutes. Drain well.

Cabbage Trim off outer leaves, quarter cabbage, then shred, removing central core. Boil for 5-7 minutes; drain well, swirl with melted butter and grated black pepper.

Carrots Scrub tender carrots; scrape or peel older ones. Leave small carrots whole; halve, quarter, slice or dice larger ones. Boil in water to cover for 5-30 minutes until tender.

Cauliflower Break into florets, trim off tough stems. Boil for 3-5 minutes, drain very well. Or steam for 8-10 minutes. Serve plainly or tossed in butter or soured cream; or coat in batter, as for salsify fritters (page 56); or cover with a cheese sauce, top with crumbs and bake until golden.

Celeriac Peel fairly thickly, cut into even sized chunks. Boil in a stainless steel or enamel pan for 30-40 minutes. Serve with butter or make into a purée (page 32).

Celery Choose small compact hearts and wash them well. Trim to

9

about 15 cm (6 in), halve or quarter lengthwise. Or use outer stalks of celery only; trim and cut into even-sized lengths. Best braised, as on page 34.

Chicory Remove damaged leaves, trim base. Insert the point of a knife in the base and twist to remove a cone-shaped 'core'; this reduces bitterness and also ensures even cooking. Cook as described for artichokes (page 15), omitting the sauce.

Chinese cabbage, Chinese leaves Trim, shred finely and stir-fry as described on page 35.

Courgettes Top and tail finger-sized courgettes, slice, dice or coarsely grate older ones. Fry in butter; or boil until barely tender, drain well and serve with butter and herbs.

Cucumber Peel and cut into 1 cm (½ in) slices, braise as described on page 34.

Fennel Trim off stalk ends, base and any tough outer leaves. Boil and serve with butter or braise, as described for celery on page 34.

French beans Top and tail; leave whole or cut large ones into shorter lengths, then boil for 2-10 minutes, depending on size.

Kale Remove stalks, pulling leaves away from stem. Boil for 5-7 minutes; drain well.

Kohlrabi Looks and sounds more exciting than it tastes. Prepare and cook as for swede.

Leeks Cut off roots and most of green part; slit down one side and rinse out grit. Leave whole, or slice. Cook as described for artichokes on page 15 or boil until tender: 1-2 minutes for sliced leeks, 8-10 minutes for thin whole leeks. Drain well.

Lettuce Prepare and cook firm, hearty lettuces as for chicory, but no need to 'core'.

Mangetout peas Prepare as for French beans. Stir-fry or boil for 2-3 minutes: they should still be slightly crunchy.

Marrow Cut off stem, halve, peel and cut marrow into even-sized pieces. Remove seeds if tough. Cook as described for artichokes (page 15).

Mushrooms Peel wild mushrooms; wash but don't peel cultivated ones. Leave small ones whole, slice large ones. Trim stalks off flat open mushrooms. Fry in butter or oil until tender. If they give off a little liquid, increase heat and cook rapidly until it disappears; if they give off a lot, drain, reserving the liquid for stock, and start again. Flat mushrooms are good brushed with oil and grilled; baby mushrooms make good fritters: follow recipe on page 56, but no need to cook the mushrooms first.

Okra Top and tail; cook gently in oil for about 20 minutes. Good fried with onions, tomatoes and spices (page 40).

Onions Bake in skins at 200°C (400°F), gas mark 6, for about 1 hour, slit and serve with butter, salt and pepper. Or peel, cut into even-sized pieces and boil for 15-45 minutes; or fry in butter or oil for about 10 minutes. For crisp onion rings, dip raw onion rings in milk and flour then deep-fry for 1-2 minutes.

Parsnips Prepare as for swede. Mash with butter and serve or make into croquettes or bake with crumbs and butter until crisp; or roast in oil (page 49).

11

Peas Shell; boil for 5-10 minutes, or braise with lettuce (page 43).

Peppers Halve, remove stalk, core and seeds. Slice, fry in oil for about 15 minutes until softened. Or fill with stuffing and bake (page 46).

Potatoes Scrape or peel potatoes, or scrub skins and leave on. Boil in water to cover until tender and serve with butter and chopped herbs, or mash with butter and milk or cream until light and fluffy. Or cook slowly in butter as described for artichokes on page 15. To bake potatoes, scrub and prick medium-sized old potatoes, rub with oil if liked, then bake at 230°C (450°F), gas mark 8, for 1-1¼ hours, until they feel soft when squeezed. Split open and eat with butter, grated cheese or soured cream. For chips, cut potatoes into slices, put one of these into a deep-frying pan one third full of fat. When it starts to sizzle add the rest and cook until golden; the longer they fry the crisper they will get. Drain and serve immediately.

Pumpkin Prepare as for marrow.

Red cabbage Prepare and cook as described on page 52.

Runner beans Top and tail; cut down the sides of beans to remove any tough strings. Cut beans into 2.5 cm (1 in) pieces or slice in a bean slicer. Boil for 5-10 minutes until just tender.

Salsify and scorzonera Scrape, keeping roots submerged. Cut into even-sized lengths, boil in water to cover in a stainless steel or enamel saucepan for 5-15 minutes, until tender. Serve with butter and herbs, in a creamy sauce or as fritters (page 56).

Spinach Wash very thoroughly. Remove stalks or keep them on, for added flavour and texture. Put spinach into a large saucepan with no extra water. As the spinach boils down, chop it with the end of a fish slice and turn it so that it cooks evenly. Drain and serve with butter, salt and black pepper.

Swede Peel thickly, cut into even-sized pieces, cover with water and boil for 15-20 minutes, until tender; or steam for 20 minutes. Mash with butter and seasoning. Delicious prepared like the parsnips on page 42 or the celeriac on page 32.

Sweet potatoes Scrub, cut into pieces and bake like potatoes, (page 47), or peel, boil and purée.

Sweetcorn Remove leaves and silky threads, trim off stalk. Immerse in large panful of boiling unsalted water, simmer for about 10 minutes, until yellow kernels are tender. Drain and serve with melted butter. To cook just the kernels, cut these from the husk then cook in boiling water for 2-5 minutes.

Swiss chard Strip leaves from stems and cook as for spinach. Cut stems into 10 cm (4 in) lengths, boil for 4-5 minutes, until just tender. Drain and serve with melted butter or a creamy sauce.

Tomatoes Remove stalks, cut a cross in the top of the tomatoes and bake at 180°C (350°F), gas mark 4, for 10-15 minutes. Or halve and fry on both sides; or halve, season, dot with butter and bake or grill for 10 minutes. Delicious stuffed (page 58).

Turnips Peel; leave baby turnips whole; halve or quarter larger ones. Boil for 5-10 minutes, drain well, return to pan and dry out over heat. Or steam 10-15 minutes. Serve with butter or as a purée, or diced and mixed with diced carrots.

Jerusalem Artichokes in Fresh Tomato Sauce

You can use canned tomatoes for this sauce, but it's worth using fresh ones if possible as they give the best flavour.

SERVES 4

700 g (1½ lb) Jerusalem
   artichokes
15g (½ oz) butter

4 tablespoons water
sea salt

For the tomato sauce
15 g (½ oz) butter
1 tablespoon oil
450 g (1 lb) tomatoes, skinned
   and chopped, *or*

1 424 g (15 oz) can tomatoes
1 clove garlic, peeled and crushed
freshly ground black pepper

First make the sauce. Heat the butter and oil in a medium-sized saucepan and add the tomatoes and garlic. Stir, then cook gently, uncovered, until reduced to a fairly thick purée: 30-40 minutes. Liquidize and season. Meanwhile peel the artichokes, and cut into even-sized chunks. Put into a heavy-based saucepan with the butter, water, and some salt and cook over a very gentle heat until just tender: 20 minutes. Pour the sauce over the artichokes and serve.

Stuffed Aubergines

These aubergines make an excellent starter or vegetarian main course, with vegetables and homemade tomato sauce.

SERVES 4

2 medium-sized aubergines
sea salt
4-6 tablespoons olive oil
1 onion, peeled and chopped
225 g (8 oz) mushrooms,
    washed and chopped

4 tablespoons chopped parsley
125 g (4 oz) curd cheese
50 g (2 oz) soft breadcrumbs
50 g (2 oz) grated cheese
freshly ground black pepper

Halve aubergines lengthwise, scoop out the centres. Sprinkle scooped-out aubergine and insides of skins with salt, put under a weight and leave for about 30 minutes. Then rinse.

Set oven to 180°C (350°F), gas mark 4. Fry aubergine skins on both sides in 3-4 tablespoons oil for 2-3 minutes. Put into a shallow ovenproof dish, then fry the onion, aubergine flesh and mushrooms, for 5 minutes, adding more oil if necessary. Add parsley, curd cheese, breadcrumbs and grated cheese; season. Spoon into aubergine skins and bake, uncovered, for about 40 minutes.

Aubergine Bake

One of my favourite aubergine dishes, this is delicious with crusty bread or buttery brown rice and a salad.

SERVES 4

700 g (1½ lb) aubergines
sea salt
flour
oil for shallow-frying
1 425 g (15 oz) can tomatoes

2 cloves garlic, peeled and
    crushed
175 g (6 oz) grated cheese
freshly ground pepper

Cut aubergines into thin strips, sprinkle with salt and leave in a colander with a weight on top for 30 minutes. Then rinse aubergines and squeeze as dry as possible. Set the oven to 190°C (375°F), gas mark 5. Dip the aubergines in flour then shallow-fry them in the oil until crisp on both sides and soft in the middle. Drain on kitchen paper. Liquidize together the tomatoes and the garlic; season with salt and pepper. Layer the aubergine slices and cheese in a shallow oven-proof dish; pour the tomato mixture evenly on top. Bake uncovered, towards the top of the oven, for 50-60 minutes, until browned and bubbling.

Beansprout Stir-fry

The beauty of this dish is the speed with which it can be cooked. It has a crunchy texture and fresh flavour.

SERVES 4

bunch of spring onions
2 carrots
1 small turnip
225 g (8 oz) Chinese leaves
350 g (12 oz) beansprouts
2 tablespoons oil (sesame oil has a
  good flavour)

1 tablespoon soy sauce
½ teaspoon sugar
sea salt and freshly ground
  black pepper

Wash, trim and chop the spring onions; scrape the carrots, peel the turnip and cut both into tiny dice. Wash and shred the Chinese leaves; soak the beansprouts in cold water for 10 minutes then drain. All this can be done ahead of time.

When you're ready to eat, heat the oil in a large saucepan or wok. Put in all the prepared vegetables and stir-fry over a high heat for 1-2 minutes, until heated through but still crisp. Add the soy sauce, sugar and some salt and pepper to taste; mix briefly then serve.

Stir-fried Broccoli with Fresh Ginger and Almonds

This is an excellent way of preparing broccoli to make the most of its vivid green colour and crunchy texture. It's very quick to do and the ginger gives a pleasant tang; not hot, more like very aromatic lemon rind.

SERVES 4

700 g (1½ lb) broccoli
piece of fresh ginger the size of a
small walnut
2 tablespoons vegetable oil

sea salt and freshly ground
black pepper
25 g (1 oz) flaked or slivered
almonds

Wash the broccoli and cut off the thick stems — you can only use the tender part for this recipe as the cooking time is so short. Cut the broccoli into small pieces, slicing the stem pieces thinly and diagonally. Peel and finely grate the ginger. Just before you want to eat, heat the oil in a large saucepan or wok. Put in the broccoli, ginger and a little salt and pepper and stir-fry for 2-3 minutes, until the broccoli has heated through and softened a little. Sprinkle with the almonds and serve at once.

Hot Beetroot in Apple Sauce

Beetroot makes a delicious cooked vegetable and can be very quick and easy if you buy ready-cooked beetroot (but not the kind that has been prepared in vinegar). In this recipe the beetroot is peeled, cubed and then gently heated in a lightly spiced apple sauce.

SERVES 4

450 g (1 lb) cooking apples
2 tablespoons water
¼-½ teaspoon ground cloves

1-2 tablespoons sugar
450 g (1 lb) cooked beetroot
sea salt

Peel, core and slice the apples; put into a medium-sized saucepan with the water and cook over a gentle heat, with a lid on the saucepan, for about 10 minutes, until soft and mushy. Mash with a spoon and mix in the ground cloves and just enough sugar to take off the sharpness. This can all be done ahead of time if convenient.

Skin the beetroot, then cut it into chunky pieces. Add these to the sauce, together with some salt, and re-heat gently.

Festive Sprouts

Here is a recipe to try if you dislike soggy, overcooked Brussels sprouts. These could not be more different; they are stir-fried for the minimum of time, retaining all their flavour and crispness and making a cheerful vegetable mixture for a winter's day.

SERVES 4

700 g (1½ lb) small, firm
   Brussels sprouts
175 g (6 oz) carrots
1 small red pepper,
   about 125 g (4 oz)

3 spring onions
1½ tablespoons oil
4-6 tablespoons water
sea salt and freshly ground
   black pepper

Wash, trim and slice the Brussels sprouts; scrape the carrots and cut into small dice; wash, de-seed and chop the red pepper; wash, trim and slice the onions. Just before you want to eat, heat the oil in a large saucepan or wok. Put in the vegetables and stir-fry for 3-4 minutes, until they have heated through and softened a little. Add the water, a little at a time, if the mixture shows signs of burning. Season with salt and pepper and serve immediately.

Purée of Brussels Sprouts

A light, buttery purée is a good way of serving the larger Brussels sprouts, particularly towards the end of the season when they're cheap and plentiful but you're tired of them. For a less rich version you can use a little of the cooking liquid or some milk instead of some or all of the cream.

SERVES 4-6

700g (1½ lb) Brussels sprouts
15 g (½ oz) butter
150 ml (5 fl oz) single cream

sea salt and freshly ground
   black pepper
nutmeg

Wash and trim the sprouts, then cook them in a little fast-boiling salted water for about 10 minutes, until they are tender. Drain the sprouts thoroughly, then pass the sprouts through a mouli-légumes or purée them in a food processor. Put the purée back into the saucepan and add the butter, then beat in enough cream to make a soft purée. Season with salt, freshly ground black pepper and grated nutmeg. Reheat gently.

Cabbage with Turmeric, Cashew Nuts and Raisins

In this recipe, the cabbage is stir-fried with turmeric and the result is golden and spicy.

SERVES 4

700 g (1½ lb) firm white cabbage
2 tablespoons oil
1 teaspoon turmeric
2 tablespoons desiccated coconut
15 g (½ oz) raisins
50 g (2 oz) broken cashew nuts
sea salt and freshly ground
   black pepper

Wash the cabbage and shred fairly finely, removing the coarse leaves and stems. Just before you want to eat the meal heat the oil and turmeric in a large saucepan or wok; put in the cabbage and stir-fry for 2½-3 minutes, until the cabbage has softened and reduced but is still crisp. Stir in the coconut, raisins and cashew nuts. Season to taste and serve immediately.

Cabbage Stuffed with Tomatoes and Walnuts and Baked in a Cheese Sauce

Served with potatoes baked in their jackets, this makes a warming and very economical meal.

SERVES 4

8 outer leaves of cabbage (savoy, Primo or January King)
1 onion, peeled and chopped
2 tablespoons oil
125 g (4 oz) walnuts, chopped
125 g (4 oz) soft breadcrumbs
1 425 g (15 oz) can tomatoes

salt and freshly ground pepper
300 ml (½ pint) cheese sauce, made from 25 g (1 oz) butter, 25 g (1 oz) flour, 275 ml (½ pint) milk, 50 g (2 oz) grated cheese
50 g (2 oz) grated cheese

Set oven to 190°C (375°F), gas mark 5. Put the cabbage leaves into a saucepan of boiling water for 2-3 minutes, until pliable. Drain well. Fry the onion in the oil for 10 minutes, add the nuts, breadcrumbs, tomatoes and seasoning. Divide mixture between the cabbage leaves, roll them up and place in a greased shallow dish. Cover with the sauce. Sprinkle with cheese and bake for 40-45 minutes.

Carrots Cooked in Butter
with Lemon and Parsley

The tender young carrots of early summer are best for this recipe, but it also works well for older carrots, cut into matchsticks.

SERVES 4

700 g (1½ lb) carrots,
    preferably small ones
15 g (½ oz) butter
150 ml (5 fl oz) water
2-3 teaspoons sugar

a squeeze of lemon juice
sea salt
freshly ground black pepper
1 tablespoon chopped fresh
    parsley

Trim and scrape the carrots, halve or quarter larger ones. Put the butter, water, 2 teaspoons sugar and ½ teaspoon salt into a medium-sized saucepan and heat until the butter has melted, then add the carrots and bring up to the boil. Cover saucepan, reduce heat and leave for 25-30 minutes, until carrots are tender. Then take the lid off the saucepan, turn up the heat and let the liquid bubble away until there is hardly any left. Add lemon juice and salt, pepper and sugar to taste. Sprinkle with chopped parsley.

Carrots in Coconut Cream Sauce with Fresh Coriander

In this recipe tender carrots are bathed in a golden sauce of coconut cream and turmeric and garnished with fresh green coriander. The flavour is spicy without being hot, making it an ideal accompaniment to curries and spiced rice dishes.

SERVES 4

700 g (1½ lb) carrots, cut in rings
25 g (1 oz) coconut cream:
  from health shops
150 ml (5 fl oz) water
1 teaspoon turmeric
sea salt and freshly ground
  black pepper

sugar
a squeeze of lemon juice
1 tablespoon chopped fresh
  coriander or parsley

Put the carrots into a medium-sized, heavy-based saucepan with the coconut cream, water and turmeric. Bring up to the boil, stir, then cover, reduce heat and leave for 10-15 minutes, until carrots are practically tender. Then turn up heat, boil uncovered, until almost all liquid has evaporated. Add sugar, lemon juice and seasoning and sprinkle with chopped coriander or parsley.

Cauliflower in Soured Cream and Tarragon Sauce

SERVES 4

1 medium-sized firm white
  cauliflower

sea salt

For the sauce
15 g (½ oz) butter
2 rounded teaspoons flour
150 ml (5 fl oz) water
1 150 ml (5 fl oz) carton
  soured cream

1 tablespoon chopped fresh
  tarragon
freshly ground black pepper

Trim cauliflower and divide into florets. Cook in 1 cm (½ in) boiling salted water until *just* tender when pierced with the point of a sharp knife. Drain well.

Meanwhile make the sauce. Melt the butter in a small saucepan and add the flour. Stir over a gentle heat until the flour bubbles, then add the water and stir until thick. Cook gently for 5 minutes, then remove from heat; mix in the soured cream, tarragon and seasoning to taste, and reheat. Serve the cauliflower with the sauce spooned over the top.

Golden Spiced Cauliflower

The cauliflower in this recipe comes out a pretty shade of gold, because of the turmeric, and it's lightly and delicately spiced.

SERVES 4

1 medium-sized cauliflower
2 tablespoons oil
2 teaspoons turmeric
4 cardamom pods
4 cloves
1 bay leaf

small piece cinnamon stick
1 clove garlic, peeled and crushed
sea salt and freshly ground
   black pepper
150 ml (5 fl oz) water

Trim cauliflower and divide into florets. Heat the oil in a medium-sized saucepan and fry the spices and bay leaf for 1-2 minutes, stirring. Add cauliflower, garlic, seasoning and water. Bring up to the boil, then simmer gently, uncovered and stirring often, for 5-7 minutes, until cauliflower is just tender and most of the liquid absorbed. Check seasoning, remove bay leaf, cinnamon and cardamom, then serve.

31

Celeriac Purée

A purée of celeriac is useful for serving instead of a sauce with dishes which need something moist to go with them. You can make this mixture rich and creamy for serving with a fairly plain main dish; or just mash the vegetables with some of their cooking water and add plenty of butter and freshly ground black pepper.

SERVES 4

450 g (1 lb) celeriac
225 g (8 oz) potatoes
15 g (½ oz) butter
up to 150 ml (5 fl oz) single cream
    or milk - optional

sea salt and freshly ground black
    pepper

Peel the celeriac and potatoes, cut them into even-sized pieces and boil them in water to cover until tender. Drain thoroughly, keeping the water. Mash with a potato masher, electric hand whisk or in a food processor. Put the mixture back into the saucepan set over a low heat. Add the butter and gradually beat in enough cream, milk or reserved cooking water to make a light, fluffy mixture, softer than mashed potatoes. Season with plenty of salt and freshly ground black pepper.

Chinese Cabbage
with Spring Onions

If you prepare the cabbage and spring onions in advance and keep them in a polythene bag in the fridge, this dish can be made very quickly, in about 5 minutes, just before the meal.

SERVES 4

1 Chinese cabbage, about 700-900 g (1½-2 lb)	sea salt and freshly ground black pepper
1 large bunch spring onions	sugar
2 tablespoons oil	
1 tablespoon chopped fresh parsley	

Wash the cabbage and shred it—not too finely. Wash, trim and chop the spring onions, keeping as much of the green part as seems reasonable. All this can be done in advance. Just before the meal, heat the oil in a fairly large saucepan and add the cabbage and spring onions. Turn them in the oil, over a fairly high heat, for about 2 minutes, until the cabbage has softened just a little but is still crisp. Add the chopped parsley and some salt, pepper and perhaps a dash of sugar to taste. Serve at once.

Braised Celery with Chestnuts

The little celery hearts which you can sometimes buy now are ideal for this recipe, though you could use a normal-size head of celery. In this case 2 heads would be enough, sliced down into quarters.

SERVES 4

4 celery hearts
15 g (½ oz) butter
1 small onion, peeled and sliced
½ bay leaf
1 283 g (10 oz) can whole
  chestnuts in water *or*
125 g (4 oz) fresh cooked
  chestnuts

sea salt and freshly ground
  black pepper
a little chopped parsley

Set oven to 180°C (350°F), gas mark 4. Wash and trim celery hearts, and slice each in half lengthwise. Melt the butter in a flameproof casserole and add the onion, celery and bay leaf. Drain chestnuts, reserving liquid. If necessary make up to 100 ml (4 fl oz) with water or stock; add to the celery, with the chestnuts and seasoning. Bring to the boil, cover and bake for 1-1¼ hours, until celery is tender. Sprinkle with chopped parsley.

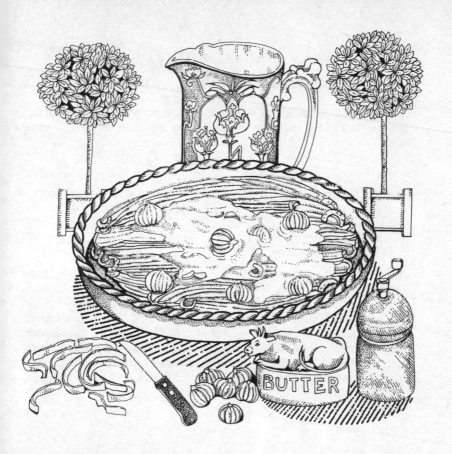

Leeks Cooked with Tomatoes and Coriander Seeds

This mixture of leeks and tomatoes, flavoured with aromatic coriander seeds, is really delicious, and it's good cold, as a starter, as well as hot.

SERVES 4

900 g (2 lb) leeks
2 tablespoons oil
1 clove garlic, crushed
450 g (1 lb) tomatoes,
    skinned and chopped

2-3 teaspoons whole coriander
    seeds, coarsely crushed
sea salt and freshly ground black
    pepper

Trim the roots and most of the leafy green tops off the leeks, then slit the leeks down one side and wash carefully under cold water. Cut into 2-cm (1-in) pieces. Heat the oil in a medium-sized saucepan and put in the garlic, tomatoes, leeks, coriander, half a teaspoon of salt and a grating of black pepper. Stir so that everything is well mixed, then leave to cook gently, without a lid, for 20-30 minutes, until the leeks are very tender and the tomatoes have formed a sauce around them. Stir quite often during the cooking time. Check the seasoning before serving.

Spicy Marrow with Ginger

The idea for this recipe came to me when I was thinking of one of the traditional uses for marrow—marrow and ginger jam. Why not make a savoury version, I thought, which would make an interesting accompanying vegetable?

SERVES 4

1 medium-sized marrow,
  about 700-900 g (1½-2 lb)
1 onion, peeled and chopped
2 tablespoons oil
1-2 teaspoons ground ginger
50 g (2 oz) crystallized or
  stem ginger, chopped

sea salt and freshly ground
  black pepper
chopped fresh coriander or
  parsley

Peel marrow, then cut into even-sized pieces about 2.5 cm (1 in) long and 6 mm (¼ in) thick: don't remove the seeds if tender. Fry the onion in oil in a medium-sized heavy based saucepan for 5 minutes. Add marrow and ground and chopped ginger. Cover and cook gently for 15-20 minutes, until marrow is nearly tender. Then take off the lid and let the mixture boil for 5-10 minutes until the liquid has evaporated. Season and sprinkle with chopped coriander or parsley.

Marrow in Tomato Sauce with Coriander and Green Peppercorns

Here, marrow is cooked in a tomato sauce enlivened with onion, coriander seed and green peppercorns. The result is spicy and delicious.

SERVES 4

1 medium-sized marrow,
   about 700-900 g (1½-2 lb)
1 onion, peeled and chopped
2 tablespoons oil
2 tablespoons tomato purée
2 teaspoons coriander seeds,
   coarsely crushed

1 teaspoon green peppercorns
sea salt and freshly ground
   black pepper
½-1 teaspoon sugar

Prepare marrow as in previous recipe. Fry the onion in the oil in a medium-sized saucepan for 5 minutes, then add the marrow, tomato purée, coriander, green peppercorns and seasoning. Stir, cover and leave over a gentle heat for 15-20 minutes, until the marrow is nearly tender. Then remove lid and boil for 5-10 minutes until the liquid has evaporated. Check seasoning, add sugar to taste.

Baby Onions in a
Cream and Nutmeg Sauce

This is a lovely creamy vegetable dish, delicately flavoured with nutmeg. If you can find baby onions, usually sold as 'pickling onions', they're ideal for this recipe, and worth the effort of peeling them. But you can also make it with larger onions cut into quarters or eighths.

SERVES 4

700 g (1½ lb) baby onions
sea salt
1 150 ml (5 fl oz) carton
   soured cream

freshly ground black pepper
freshly grated nutmeg

Peel the onions using a sharp, pointed knife, leaving them whole if they're tiny, or cutting them into smaller sections if larger. Bring 2 cm (1 in) lightly salted water to the boil in a fairly large saucepan; add the onions, cover with a lid and boil for 7-10 minutes until the onions feel just tender when pierced with a sharp knife. Drain well, then put the onions back into the saucepan and stir in the soured cream and some salt, pepper and nutmeg to taste. Heat gently for a minute or two, stirring all the time, but don't let the mixture get too near boiling point or the cream may separate. Serve at once.

Spiced Okra

I love the glutinous texture of okra. It's especially good as a side dish with curries, but would go well with many plain dishes.

SERVES 4 AS A SIDE DISH, 2 AS A MAIN DISH WITH RICE

1 small onion, peeled and
    chopped
1 clove garlic, peeled and crushed
2 tablespoons oil
1 teaspoon ground cumin
1 teaspoon ground coriander
2 tomatoes, skinned and chopped
250 g (8 oz) okra, washed and
    trimmed

4 tablespoons water
1 tablespoon tomato purée
sea salt and freshly ground
    black pepper
a little sugar

Fry the onion and garlic in the oil for 5 minutes without letting them brown, then stir in the spices, tomatoes, okra, water, the tomato purée and 1 teaspoonful of salt. Stir well, then put a lid on the saucepan and leave to cook over a gentle heat for 20 minutes, stirring from time to time. The okra should feel tender when pierced with a pointed knife. Check the seasoning and add a dash of sugar to bring out the flavour if necessary.

Curried Parsnip Cream

My original idea was to cook and mash the parsnips then make them into a savoury bake. However they tasted so good when they'd been mashed with some curry powder and cream that I decided it would be a pity to do anything more to them!

SERVES 4

700 g (1½ lb) parsnips
1 onion, peeled and chopped
15 g (½ oz) butter
2 teaspoons mild curry powder

150 ml (5 fl oz) cream or
  top-of-the-milk
salt and freshly ground pepper
a few chopped walnuts

Peel the parsnips and cut them into even-sized chunks, removing any hard core. Put them into a saucepan with boiling water to cover and cook, with a lid on the saucepan, until the parsnips are tender: 15-20 minutes. Drain.

While the parsnips are cooking, fry the onion in the butter for 7-8 minutes, until nearly tender, then stir in the curry powder and cook for a further couple of minutes.

Mash the parsnips until smooth and creamy, then beat in the onion and curry mixture, the cream and salt and pepper to taste. Serve sprinkled with the chopped walnuts.

Peas Cooked with Lettuce

This is my favourite way of cooking peas and a marvellous way of adding flavour to frozen peas.

SERVES 4

450 g (1 lb) outside leaves of lettuce, such as Webb's
450 g (1 lb) shelled weight of fresh or frozen peas (this is about 1.5 kg/3 lb peas weighed in the pod)

15 g (½ oz) butter
½ teaspoon sugar
sea salt and freshly ground black pepper

Wash the lettuce then shred it quite coarsely with a sharp knife. Put the lettuce into a heavy-based saucepan with the peas, butter, sugar and seasoning. Set the pan over a moderate heat and cook for 15-20 minutes, with a lid on the pan, until the peas are tender. Frozen peas only take about 7-10 minutes. Drain off any excess liquid which the lettuce has produced, and serve.

VARIATION

This mixture, liquidized, makes a good purée.

Peppers Stuffed with Pine Nuts Apricots and Raisins

There's a Middle-Eastern flavour to this fragrantly spiced dish.

SERVES 4

1 onion, peeled and chopped
1 clove garlic, peeled and crushed
½ teaspoon powdered cinnamon
1 tablespoon oil
350g (12 oz) cooked brown rice
50 g (2 oz) pine nuts or chopped cashew nuts
25-50 g (1-2 oz) raisins
25-50 g (1-2 oz) chopped dried apricots
sea salt and freshly ground black pepper
4 small squat red or green peppers, about 75-100 g (3-4 oz) each
1 tablespoon tomato purée
150 ml (5 fl oz) water

Fry onion, garlic and cinnamon in the oil for 4-5 minutes, then add the cooked rice, nuts, raisins and apricots; season. Set oven to 180°C (350°F), gas mark 4. Slice tops off the peppers and scoop out seeds. Stand peppers in a deep, ovenproof dish, fill them with rice mixture, and replace tops as lids. Mix tomato purée with the water, season, and pour round the peppers. Bake for 1-1½ hours.

Peperonata

This Italian pepper stew is one of those useful dishes which can take the place of a vegetable dish and a sauce, adding moisture to a meal. It is also good with spaghetti or as a filling for pancakes, and cold, as part of a salad selection.

SERVES 4

3 tablespoons olive oil
1 large onion, peeled and chopped
700 g (1½ lb) peppers, de-seeded and chopped: I like to use a mixture of red and green, and yellow too if available.

1 clove garlic, peeled and crushed
3 tomatoes, skinned, seeded and chopped
sea salt and freshly ground black pepper

Heat the oil in a large saucepan and fry the onion for 5 minutes, until beginning to soften but not brown. Add the peppers and garlic and continue to fry for a further 10 minutes, then put in the tomatoes and leave the mixture to cook gently for 10-15 minutes, until all the vegetables are soft and the mixture is fairly thick. Stir often to prevent sticking. Check seasoning, then serve.

Bircher Potatoes

In this recipe potatoes are scrubbed, cut in half and baked, cut-side down, on a greased baking tray. This means that the cut-sides get crisp and golden, like roast potatoes, while tops are like jacket-baked potatoes. This is a pleasant combination, and these potatoes are very popular with my children. They are also quick and easy to do, healthy and high in fibre. Leave out the caraway seeds if you don't like them.

SERVES 4

4 medium-sized potatoes	sea salt
butter	caraway seeds

Set the oven to 230°C (450°F), gas mark 8. Scrub the potatoes then cut each in half lengthwise. Grease a baking tray generously with butter. Place the potatoes, cut-side down, on the baking tray and sprinkle them with salt and caraway seeds. Bake for 40-50 minutes, until the tops of the potatoes feel soft when squeezed and the cut-sides are crisp and golden brown.

Gratin Dauphinois

A favourite potato dish, and one that's ideal for entertaining because it doesn't need last minute attention and will keep perfectly in a cool oven if the meal is delayed.

SERVES 4-6

40 g (1½ oz) butter or margarine
700 g (1½ lb) firm-textured
   potatoes
300 ml (10 fl oz) single cream
1 clove garlic, peeled and halved

salt and freshly ground
   black pepper
a little freshly grated
   nutmeg—optional

Grease a shallow ovenproof dish generously with half the butter or margarine. Set oven to 160°C (325°F), gas mark 3. Peel and finely slice the potatoes. Rinse well and pat dry on kitchen paper. Mix the cream with the garlic. Arrange the potato slices in the prepared dish in layers and season with salt, and pepper, and some grated nutmeg, if you like. Pour the cream and garlic mixture over them and dot with the rest of the butter. Bake, uncovered, for 1½-2 hours, until the potatoes feel tender when pierced with the point of a knife.

Golden Roast Potatoes

The important thing to remember with roast potatoes is that both the oil and the potatoes must be really hot. Start parboiling the potatoes when you put the tin of oil in the oven.

SERVES 4

700 g (1½ lb) potatoes   sea salt
oil

Set the oven to 230°C (400°F), gas mark 8. Put about 6 mm (¼ in) oil into a roasting tin and place high up in the oven to heat up. Peel the potatoes and cut them into even-sized chunky pieces. Put these into a saucepan with water to cover and parboil for 7 minutes. Drain thoroughly. Take the tin of oil out of the oven and place over the heat. Carefully put the potatoes into the oil, turning them over with a spoon so that they are coated with the oil. Put the tin back into the oven and roast the potatoes for 40-60 minutes, turning them over with a spoon once or twice during the cooking time. Drain them on kitchen paper, sprinkle with salt and serve immediately.

Pumpkin and Garlic Purée

'Is it custard?' asked one of my daughters, the first time I tried this. Used though my family are to trying strange mixtures, this was too much. I reassured them and they agreed to try this delicate mixture which is a cross between a purée and a sauce. (I did however make a mental note to try a sweet and spicy version sometime for serving with puddings.)

SERVES 4

700 g (1½ lb) pumpkin
15 g (½ oz) butter
2 cloves garlic, peeled and
   crushed

sea salt and freshly ground
   black pepper

Peel the pumpkin and remove the seeds. Boil the pumpkin in a little water for about 10 minutes until tender. Drain very well, then return to the saucepan and mash with the butter, garlic and salt and pepper to taste. Alternatively put all these ingredients into the liquidizer and blend to a smooth cream. Check seasoning, then re-heat and serve.

Ratatouille

I think it's worth using red peppers in this recipe because they give the best colour.

SERVES 6

2 large onions, peeled and chopped

450 g (1 lb) red peppers, de-sceded and sliced

3 tablespoons olive oil

2-4 large cloves garlic, peeled and crushed

450 g (1 lb) courgettes or marrow, cut into small dice

450 g (1 lb) aubergines, cut into small dice

700 g (1½ lb) tomatoes, skinned and chopped

freshly ground black pepper

chopped parsley

Fry onions and peppers in the oil in a large saucepan for 5 minutes, without browning; add the garlic, courgettes or marrow, and aubergines; stir, then cover saucepan and cook for 20-25 minutes, until all the vegetables are tender. Add tomatoes and cook, uncovered, for a further 4-5 minutes, to heat the tomatoes through. Season and sprinkle with chopped parsley. I like to serve ratatouille as a main dish in the summer with buttered rice, pasta or new potatoes.

Red Cabbage Casserole

This is good as a vegetable or on its own with jacket-baked potatoes and soured cream.

SERVES 4-6

700 g (1½-2 lb) red cabbage
3 tablespoons oil
2 large onions, peeled and
    chopped
1½ teaspoons sea salt

1 teaspoon sugar
2 tablespoons wine vinegar
½ teaspoon cinnamon
pinch ground cloves
freshly ground black pepper

Shred the cabbage with a sharp knife, cutting out and discarding any hard central core. Heat the oil in a large saucepan and fry the onions for 5-10 minutes. Then add cabbage, salt, sugar, vinegar, spices and a grating of pepper. Cover with a lid and either leave the cabbage to cook very gently, for about 1½ hours; or transfer the mixture to an ovenproof casserole, cover with a lid and bake in a warm oven, 160°C (325°F), gas mark 3, for about 2 hours. Stir the mixture from time to time to help it to cook evenly.

Runner Beans Cooked in Oil with Paprika

This is my attempt to re-create a bean dish which we ate in a little *taverna* in Greece. It was served to us just warm; it is also good chilled, as part of a salad. You can use other kinds of green beans besides runners.

SERVES 4

700 g (1½ lb) runner beans
2 tablespoons olive oil
1 tablespoon paprika pepper
pinch of cayenne pepper
small clove garlic, peeled and
   crushed

150 ml (5 fl oz) water
sea salt and freshly ground
   black pepper

Wash and top and tail the beans. Cut into diagonal slices. Heat the oil, paprika and cayenne pepper in a medium-sized saucepan, then stir in the beans and garlic. Pour in the water, bring up to the boil, cover, and leave over a gentle heat for 15 minutes. By this time the beans should be soft and there should be very little liquid left: if there is, bubble it away over a high heat. Check seasoning before serving.

Salsify Baked in a Lemon Sauce

SERVES 4-6

900 g (2 lb) salsify
salt and freshly ground pepper

For the sauce
25 g (1½ oz) butter
2 tablespoons flour
300 ml (10 fl oz) water
2 tablespoons lemon juice

300 ml (10 fl oz) soured cream
1 teaspoon Dijon mustard
fresh wholewheat crumbs and a
little butter for topping

Scrape the salsify, cut into 5 cm (2 in) lengths and cook in boiling salted water to cover, until just tender: drain and put into a lightly greased shallow gratin dish. Set the oven to 180°C (350°F), gas mark 4. Melt the butter in a small saucepan and stir in the flour; when it bubbles add the water and stir until smooth and thick. Then remove from the heat and mix in the lemon juice, soured cream and mustard, and salt and pepper to taste. Spoon the sauce over the salsify, sprinkle with breadcrumbs, dot with butter and bake for 40-45 minutes, until heated through and crisp on top.

Salsify Fritters

These delicate fritters make a perfect first course.

SERVES 4-6

700 g (1½ lb) salsify
3 tablespoons wine vinegar
1-2 tablespoons chopped fresh
  herbs

salt and freshly ground pepper

For the batter
125 g (4 oz) plain flour
1 tablespoon oil
2 eggs, separated

150 ml (5 fl oz) water
oil for deep-frying
lemon slices

Prepare and cook the salsify as described on page 55. Drain well, then sprinkle with the vinegar, herbs and some salt and pepper.

Mix together the flour, oil, seasoning, egg yolks and water; whisk the egg whites, then fold into the batter mixture.

Heat the oil to 190°C (275°F) (or when the batter sizzles if dropped into the oil). Coat salsify in batter, fry until browned. Drain and serve with lemon.

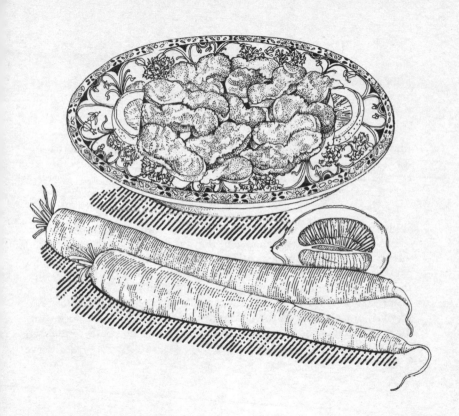

Tomatoes with Herb Stuffing

This makes a good light supper dish, perhaps served with buttered brown rice or noodles and a crisp green salad.

SERVES 4

4 large tomatoes
sea salt
125 g (4 oz) fine, soft breadcrumbs
3-4 tablespoons chopped fresh
  parsley

1 teaspoon dried mixed herbs
1 clove garlic, peeled and crushed
25 g (1 oz) butter
freshly ground black pepper

Set oven to 190°C (375°F), gas mark 5. Slice tops off tomatoes, scoop out insides with a teaspoon. Keep the scooped out tomato. Sprinkle the insides of the tomatoes with salt. Mix together the breadcrumbs, parsley, mixed herbs, half the garlic and the butter. Season with salt and pepper. Stand the tomatoes in a lightly greased, shallow, oven-proof dish and fill with the breadcrumb mixture. Liquidize the reserved tomato pulp and the slices from the tops of the tomatoes with the remaining garlic and a little salt and pepper. Pour this round the tomatoes. Bake for about 20 minutes.

Turnips in Carrot and Ginger Sauce

I devised this recipe without much enthusiasm one winter's day when I was extremely tired both of root vegetables and of cooking and couldn't think what to make. But as often happens when you just throw things together, it worked rather well: the orange sauce looks pretty over the white turnips and gives just the right touch of sweetness.

SERVES 4

700 g (1½ lb) turnips   sea salt

For the sauce

1 small onion, peeled and chopped

2 teaspoons grated fresh ginger

1 tablespoon oil

225 g (8 oz) carrots, scraped and chopped

400 ml (¾ pint) water

freshly ground black pepper

Peel turnips, cut into even-sized chunks, boil in salted water until just tender and drain. Fry the onion, ginger and carrots in the oil for 5 minutes, then add the water and simmer for about 15 minutes, until carrots are tender. Liquidize and season. Serve turnips with the sauce poured over them.

Index

Alphabetical guide to preparing and cooking vegetables 8-13
Apple sauce, hot beetroot in 22
Artichokes, globe 8
Artichokes, Jerusalem 8
in fresh tomato sauce 15
Asparagus 8
Aubergine(s) 8
bake 18
stuffed 16

Baby onions in a cream and nutmeg sauce 41
Bake, aubergine 18
Basic
cooking 6-7
preparation 5-6
Beans
broad 9
French 10
runner 12
runner, cooked in oil with paprika 54

Beansprout(s) 8
stir-fry 19
Beetroot 8
in apple sauce, hot 22
Bircher potatoes 47
Boiling vegetables 6-7
Braised celery with chestnuts 34
Broad beans 9
Broccoli 9
with fresh ginger and almonds, stir-fried 21
Brussels sprouts 9
purée of 24

Cabbage 9
Chinese 10
Chinese cabbage with spring onions 33
red 12
stuffed with tomatoes and walnuts and baked in a cheese sauce 26
with turmeric, cashewnuts and raisins 25

Calabrese 9
Carrot(s) 9
    in coconut cream sauce with fresh
        coriander 29
    and ginger sauce, turnips in 59
Casserole, red cabbage 52
Cauliflower 9
    golden spiced 31
    in soured cream and tarragon
        sauce 30
Celeriac 9
    purée 32
Celery 9-10
    braised, with chestnuts 34
Cheese sauce, cabbage stuffed with
        tomatoes and walnuts and
        baked in a 26
Chestnuts, braised celery with 34
Chicory 10
Chinese
    cabbage 10
    cabbage with spring onions 35
    leaves 10
Coconut cream sauce, carrots in,
    with fresh coriander 29
Cooking
    basic 6-7
    vegetables, an alphabetical guide
        to preparing and 8-13

Courgettes 10
Cream
    curried parsnip 42
    and nutmeg sauce, baby onions
        in 39
Cucumber 10
Curried parsnip cream 42

Dauphinois, gratin 48

Fennel 10
Festive sprouts 23
Flavouring and serving 7
French beans 10
Fritters, salsify 56

Golden
    roast potatoes 49
    spiced cauliflower 31
Gratin dauphinois 48

Herb stuffing, tomatoes with 58
Hot beetroot in apple sauce

Jerusalem artichokes 8
    in fresh tomato sauce 15

Kale 10
Kohlrabi 10

Leeks 10-11
  cooked with tomatoes and
    coriander seeds 36
Lettuce 11
  peas cooked with 43

Mangetout peas 11
Marrow 11
  spicy, with ginger 37
  in tomato sauce with coriander and
    green peppercorns 38
Mushrooms 11
  fried 11

Okra 11
  spiced 40
Onion(s) 11
  baby, in a cream and nutmeg
    sauce 39
  baked 11
  rings, crisp 11

Parsnip(s) 11
  cream, curried 42
Peas 11
  cooked with lettuce 43
  mangetout 11
Peperonata 46
Pepper(s) 12

stuffed with pine nuts, apricots
    and raisins 44
Potato(es) 12
  baked 12
  Bircher 47
  chips 12
  golden roast 49
  mashed 12
  sweet 12
Preparation, basic 5-6
Preparing and cooking vegetables, an
  alphabetical guide to 8-13
Pumpkin 12
  and garlic purée 50
Purée
  of brussels sprouts 24
  celeriac 32
  pumpkin and garlic 50

Ratatouille 51
Red cabbage 12
  casserole 52
Roast potatoes, golden 49
Runner beans 12
  cooked in oil with paprika 54

Salsify 12
  baked in a lemon sauce 55
  fritters 56

Sauce
    apple, hot beetroot in 22
    carrot and ginger, turnips in 59
    cheese, cabbage stuffed with
        tomatoes and walnuts and
        baked in a 26
    coconut cream, carrots in, with
        fresh coriander 29
    cream and nutmeg, baby onions in
        a 41
    fresh tomato, Jerusalem
        artichokes in 15
    lemon, salsify baked in 55
    soured cream and tarragon,
        cauliflower in 30
    tomato, marrow in, with coriander
        and green peppercorns 38
Scorzonera 12
Serving, flavouring and 7
Soured cream and tarragon sauce,
    cauliflower in 30
Spiced okra 40
Spicy marrow with ginger 37
Spinach 12-13
Sprouts, festive 23
Steaming 7
Stir-fried broccoli with fresh ginger
    and almonds 21
Stir-fry, beansprout 19

Stuffed
    aubergines 16
    cabbage, with walnuts and
        tomatoes, baked in a cheese
        sauce 26
    peppers, with pine nuts, apricots
        and raisins 46
Stuffing, tomatoes with herb 58
Swede 13
Sweetcorn 13
Sweet potatoes 13
Swiss chard 13

Tomato(es) 13
    baked 13
    and coriander seeds, leeks cooked
        with 36
    grilled 13
    with herb stuffing 58
    sauce, Jerusalem artichokes in
        fresh 15
    sauce, marrow in, with coriander
        and green peppercorns 38
    and walnuts, cabbage stuffed with
        and baked in a cheese sauce 36
Turmeric, cashew nuts and raisins,
    cabbage with 25
Turnips 13
    in carrot and ginger sauce 59